STEVE WOZNIAK
A WIZARD CALLED WOZ

Rebecca Gold

 Lerner Publications Company ▪ Minneapolis

This book is dedicated to Rick and Barbette Sharp and all the wonderful kids at Via Pacifica School in Manhattan Beach, CA. Especially to my 1992 "cool kids in Pod 2": Anna, BJ, Brandon, Chelsea, Daniel, Eric, Jamie, Jennie, Kristin C., Kristin H., Laura, Matt P., Matt Y., Micah, Necia, Nick, Nicole, Ryan, Steven, Susan, Vanessa, and Yolla

I would also like to thank Stephen Wozniak for taking the time to talk with me.

The cover of *Steve Wozniak* was assembled on Macintosh hardware using QuarkXPress 3.3. The graphic elements were created in Adobe Photoshop 2.5.

A glossary of computer terms
begins on page 70.

LIBRARY OF CONGRESS CATALOGING-IN-PUBLICATION DATA

Gold, Rebecca.
    Steve Wozniak : a wizard called Woz / by Rebecca Gold.
      p. cm—(Achievers)
    ISBN 0-8225-2881-9
    1. Wozniak, Stephen Gary, 1950- . 2. Microcomputers—Biography. 3. Apple computer—History. I. Title. II. Series.
QA76.2.W69G65 1994
338.7'6100416'092—dc20   94-859
[B]   CIP

Manufactured in the United States of America

1 2 3 4 5 6 – I/JR – 99 98 97 96 95 94

Contents

STEVE WOZNIAK

$H = F^3$

June 14, 1986, was a warm, sunny graduation day at the University of California at Berkeley. The dean of the engineering school stood at the podium, ready to introduce the valedictorian— the student who received the highest grades in the senior class. The audience was silent. Those who already knew who the valedictorian was nudged their neighbors and pointed.

"This is a first," the dean began. "Usually we select the person who's the most likely to succeed. This year we've done things a little backwards. Our speaker is someone who's already succeeded and made his fortune. It is with great pleasure that I introduce Mr. Rocky Raccoon Clark, better known to you, perhaps, as Stephen Wozniak."

The crowd cheered wildly. The other members of the graduating class stood up and applauded loudly. Whistles, shouts, and applause filled the air. This audience certainly knew "The Woz." Not only had he invented the first personal computer that most of the students and faculty used, but he created an entire new industry along with it. Ten years earlier, he and his teenage friend, Steve Jobs, began assembling the computer board that Woz designed—which they called the "Apple"—in Jobs's garage. They had planned to sell it at the computer club they belonged to, or maybe, if they were lucky, they'd sell a few to a local electronics store.

That venture led in 1977 to the Apple II, the first fully assembled, programmable computer small enough to fit on a desk. The Apple II required no knowledge of wiring or computer programming. It was a computer a "regular person" could use, created for (and by) a new generation.

The original Apple I computer

Soon after that, more than 20 computer companies were formed, but none achieved greater success than Apple Computer. In just six years, the company that began with two teenagers in a garage was worth more than $6 billion. Apple computers were being used almost everywhere. In just one decade, a hobbyist's dream turned into a $46-billion industry. The personal computer business became one of the largest manufacturing industries in the world and one of the greatest American business success stories.

And now here he was, a technical genius and self-made millionaire returning to college. He had used the name of his dog (Rocky Raccoon) combined with his wife's family name (Clark) so that he wouldn't receive any special attention from classmates or teachers. He wanted to complete his college degree so that he could become an elementary school teacher.

Stephen Wozniak ambled up to the podium, his head slightly bowed, his cheeks flushed. Recognition and fame wasn't exactly new to him, but he still had a hard time getting used to it. And he still doubted that he deserved it all. Often he would say, "I just built a computer because I couldn't afford to buy one. That's all."

Woz addressed the audience in his typical, humble way. He smiled, looked out at the 500 people anxiously awaiting his words, and took a deep breath. Then he spoke, softly and clearly, into the microphone.

"Happiness is the only thing life's about," he said. "You don't buy a computer unless you think it's a road to greater happiness. You don't do anything in life unless it's for happiness. That's the only way you can measure life, by the number of smiles per day." He paused. The audience was silent. "That's my theorem of life," he continued. "A simple formula, really: $H = F^3$. Happiness equals food, fun, and friends."

Nothing was more important to Stephen Wozniak. Fame and fortune weren't part of his formula. "I never started out trying to pursue money," he would often say. "I knew I was going to be happy telling jokes all my life."

After the graduation ceremony, Woz and a group of friends and family members went to a local pizza parlor to celebrate. As a joke, one of his close friends smashed a pie in Woz's face and took a picture for the newspaper. The caption read, **"Stephen Wozniak—Computer Pie-In-Ear."**

Stephen Wozniak can truly be called a pioneer of his time. His contributions shaped a new and exciting world of computers we may never have known without him.

The Wiz Kid

Stephen Wozniak was fascinated by electronics from the time he was a young boy. His family moved to northern California in 1957 when he was just seven years old, and they couldn't have chosen a more perfect place. The Santa Clara valley was in the midst of an electronics revolution and quickly came to be known as "the electronics capital of the world." New companies were opening daily, making exciting discoveries in technology and manufacturing new electronic devices.

One of the most significant technological breakthroughs came in the late 1950s with the invention of the transistor. A transistor is made from a tiny slice of crystal from a natural element in the earth (such as silicon, which comes from sand). The crystal has the ability to conduct an electrical charge. Before the invention of the transistor, computers worked by using vacuum tubes to generate electricity. In 1955, William Shockley, one of the three scientists who invented the transistor, started a company called Shockley Semiconductors to build transistors. Within a few years, several other companies were formed to build transistors, most located within a few miles of Palo Alto, California, where Shockley was located. Since by this time nearly all transistors were made of silicon, the area came to be known as the Silicon Valley.

Stephen Wozniak loved living so close to companies discovering and manufacturing exciting new electronic devices. He quickly earned the nickname "Woz the Wiz" (or simply "Woz") because of his numerous electronic inventions.

Jerry Wozniak, Stephen's father, was also an electronics buff. He studied electrical engineering at California Institute of Technology in Pasadena.

Early computers, such as the IBM System/360 Model 50, were large enough to fill an entire room.

Margret Wozniak, Steve's mother, grew up on a small farm in Washington State and had spent a summer during World War II working as a shipyard electrician. For several years, Jerry and Margret Wozniak traveled around southern California, where Jerry worked for several different aerospace companies. Their first son, Stephen Gary Wozniak, was born on August 11, 1950, in San Jose, California.

Jerry Wozniak worked long hours and would often bring work home at night. Stephen became interested from a very early age in reading the engineering literature his father brought with him.

Woz discovered reading at age three and has loved books ever since.

Woz (at left), age six, with his brother, Mark, and his sister, Leslie.

If Christmas toys had to be assembled, Stephen could usually put the pieces together without help from any written instructions (or from his parents).

When Stephen was seven years old, Lockheed Corporation persuaded Jerry Wozniak to move with his family to a town called Sunnyvale in the Santa Clara valley of northern California. Lockheed made components for the *Discoverer, Explorer, Mercury,* and *Gemini* space satellites. The company wanted Jerry to work in its new Missile Systems Division on some secret projects that involved making electronic components as small as possible. Jerry and Margret thought the move to Sunnyvale would be good for their family, which now included seven-year-old Stephen, his five-year-old sister, Leslie, and his three-year-old brother, Mark.

Stephen had a happy childhood in Sunnyvale. He was never at a loss for something to do. He went to school in the neighboring town of Cupertino and was for the most part a good student, although he was often more interested in playing the perfect practical joke on a classmate (or even the teacher or school principal)! He enjoyed sports—tennis and swimming in particular—and played Little League baseball on a team coached by his father. He and his father also played tennis in a father-son league every Saturday morning and once won a tournament together.

The Wozniak family had a lot of pets, including Mertyl the Turtle, Hercules the Rat, and Leonard and Lolita, mice who gave birth to many, many more. The mice were Stephen's favorite, and he loved to take them out of their cage and let them roam free in the house. Several years later Stephen developed an allergy to mice, which caused severe asthma attacks.

Stephen liked to watch science fiction TV shows, such as *The Twilight Zone* and *The Outer Limits,* and spy shows such as *The Man from*

U.N.C.L.E. and *I Spy.* Spy shows were a particular favorite of Stephen's, possibly because of all the secretive projects going on at Lockheed. Many of the neighborhood kids' dads also worked at Lockheed. Stephen and his friends wanted to start a top-secret spy agency to keep a close watch on the neighbors they suspected were Russian spies.

Fishing and Little League baseball were just two of the sports Woz loved as a kid.

But Stephen's favorite pastime of all was designing and building electronic projects for science fairs or just for his own enjoyment. He was lucky to live in a neighborhood filled with engineers and electronics enthusiasts who were ready and able to answer questions or offer advice. His next-door neighbor Alfred Taylor owned an electronics store in town. Mr. Taylor traded spare or broken electronic parts with the children in the neighborhood in exchange for mowing his lawn or doing odd jobs. Stephen and his good friend Bill Fernendez could often be found in Mr. Taylor's yard, scrambling around for electronic parts that looked interesting enough for experiments.

Another neighbor offered lessons to people who wanted to obtain licenses for operating amateur, or ham, radios. This inspired 12-year-old Stephen to build his own 100-watt ham radio and take the lessons and the operator's exam. Stephen passed the exam the first time he took it, and his father installed an antenna on their roof so that Stephen could use his ham radio to communicate with other ham radio operators around the world. Woz preferred, however, to use his ham radio to communicate with his neighborhood friends. He wired speakers in their homes so they could talk to each other late at night when they were supposed to be in bed sleeping.

Woz learned to operate a ham radio at age 11.

For a seventh-grade science project, Stephen created an electronic tic-tac-toe game. He hammered nails into one side of a board to connect the necessary electronic parts, then he hooked up red and white light bulbs on the other side in the shape of a tic-tac-toe game. On the bottom of the board, he placed a row of switches that allowed a player to select a move. Stephen wired the circuits so that after a player selected a move, the machine would try and outsmart its opponent.

Stephen loved to read books and magazines about electronics and computers. Often he would write to a company and ask for more information, and if he was lucky the company would send him very technical books and detailed diagrams of their products. Little did they know the person at the other end of the request was in junior high school. While some of Stephen's classmates may have had pictures of famous athletes or musical groups on their bedroom walls, Stephen decorated his room with pictures of the latest computers and electronics magazine covers!

One day when Stephen was 12 years old, he saw—in a book about computers—a diagram that changed his life. The diagram showed a simple calculator called the One Bit Adder-Subtracter, which could add or subtract numbers one digit at a time. Stephen understood most of the diagram, but there were some parts he had never seen before. Through this diagram, he discovered that electronic switches could be used to represent statements that were true or false. For example, if an electronic switch was on, it could mean a particular statement is true. If it was off, the statement was false. Electronic components could be used to show logical operations! This was an exciting discovery for Stephen. It prompted him to build a machine that was 10 times faster than the one he'd seen in the book. He called his creation the Ten Bit Parallel Adder-Subtracter. It could add or subtract numbers up to 10 digits at a time. Stephen designed the circuits by himself and placed the necessary electrical components on a small board. The board had two rows of switches on the bottom—one for adding, the other for subtracting. The solution to an arithmetic problem was displayed on the bottom row of lights.

Stephen's Ten Bit Parallel Adder-Subtracter machine was his first simple computer. He proudly entered it into the Cupertino School District science fair and won first place. He also entered it in the Bay Area science fair, competing against students at least four years older, and won third place. As a reward, he was taken on his first trip in an airplane over California's Alameda Naval Air Station. Stephen was thrilled and decided then that someday he would fly his own airplane.

By the time Stephen entered Cupertino's Homestead High School in 1964, there were two things that most interested him. Electronics was number one, and playing practical jokes every chance he got ran a close second. He started out with simple pranks—setting all the clocks in the school one hour ahead or putting notes on classroom doors that led students (and teachers) to the wrong room. It didn't take long, however, for him to combine his love of electronics with his love for practical jokes!

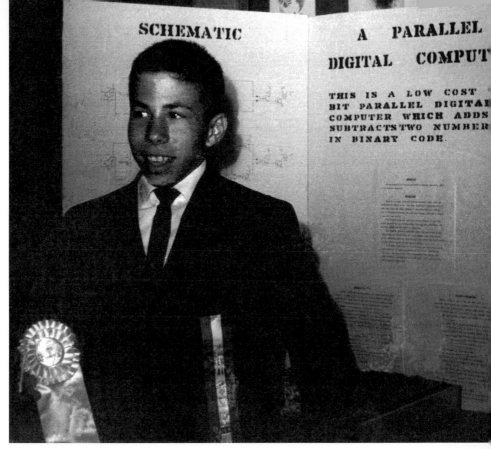

Woz won first place at the Bay Area science fair.

Once he built an electronic device that could set off the school's fire alarm. Another time he used part of an old battery, an oscillator (an electronic instrument that makes a ticking noise), and some wires to create something that looked like a bomb. Without being seen, he put it in a friend's locker. The ticking of the oscillator soon attracted attention, and the school's principal was called in a panic to disarm the "bomb." The principal held the device at arm's length, walked very carefully out into the middle of the school's football field and put it down, waiting for the emergency bomb squad to arrive. The bomb squad soon found that the device was a fake, and the principal knew right away who was behind the joke. Woz thought his prank was terrific, as did his classmates, who gave him a standing ovation for his joke. His parents, however, didn't think it was so funny when their son was suspended from school for two days and taken to juvenile hall to spend the night in jail.

Besides being the school's number-one prankster, Woz was also the number-one student in his electronics class. He was president of both the electronics and math clubs. His electronics teacher, John McCollum, quickly realized that high school electronics was no challenge for Woz. He worked out an arrangement with a nearby company, GTE/Sylvania Electronics, for Woz and his friend Alan Baum to spend every Wednesday afternoon in the company's computer room. That room contained the first big computer Stephen ever saw, a mainframe called the IBM 1130. The 1130 was about the size of a refrigerator. It shook the floor when it operated, and it was so loud that people had to shout to be heard over the loud humming noise. To enter information into the computer, an operator punched holes in cards using a special keyboard machine and fed the cards into the computer one at a time. If one card contained the slightest error, the whole procedure had to be started all over again.

The GTE engineers were patient and helped the boys understand how the system worked. Woz and Alan learned all about software—the programs necessary to make a computer work. Woz quickly learned how to write simple programs the computer could understand. Soon he was writing programs to calculate moves on a chessboard or solve difficult math problems. Woz learned so much at GTE that sometimes McCollum invited him to give lectures to the electronics class at Homestead High School.

Alan Baum's father worked at the Stanford Research Institute and sometimes allowed the boys to spend time in the computer room there. One of the machines the boys learned about at Stanford was the PDP-8, made by Digital Electronics Corporation. The PDP-8 was a new type of computer called a "minicomputer." Minicomputers were smaller and faster than mainframe computers. Woz was completely intrigued. He read the PDP-8 manual from cover to cover. Soon he was drawing plans for his own version of the PDP-8. The more he read, the more he wanted to have a computer of his very own.

24

The Cream Soda Computer

Stephen Wozniak graduated from Homestead High School in 1968 with high honors. He was a member of the National Honor Society and the California Scholarship Federation and was listed in *Who's Who in American High Schools* for achievements in math and electronics. He received four scholarship awards in math and electronics, a grant from the National Science Foundation, a cash award from the Mount Diablo Computer Programming Contest, and a savings bond from the National High School Math Contest. He also received a perfect score in math on his college entrance exams. Woz, however, was far more proud of his high school pranks than he was of his academic record!

By the time Woz graduated from high school, two months before his 18th birthday, he had designed on paper more than 50 computers. He was sure the machines would work. The only thing that stopped him from building them was the cost of the necessary components.

Jerry Wozniak wanted Stephen to attend the same college he went to—California Institute of Technology, in Pasadena. Stephen, however, wanted to live in Colorado, where he had recently seen snow for the first time. He decided to attend the University of Colorado in Boulder. He wasn't quite ready for college-level schoolwork, though, and spent most of his time in the school's computer lab or playing bridge. He continued to be a first-rate practical joker. One of his favorite jokes involved a frequency jammer—a little device he built that disrupted the reception of a television set. The device was so small it could be disguised as an ordinary pen! When a television show reached a crucial scene, Woz would quietly click on the little device, and the picture would disappear. Once he clicked the jammer just as the winner of the Kentucky Derby was about to cross the finish line. Woz managed to conceal his laughter pretty well, as he watched his friends fiddle with the TV antenna and stand in all sorts of awkward positions thinking that would keep the reception clear!

After a year of college, Woz found he was no longer interested in pursuing academics. He just wanted to get on with his computer projects, so he decided to return to Sunnyvale, where he could be around the electronics action once again. That summer, he and his friend Alan Baum, who had

The University of Colorado in Boulder

just finished his freshman year at the Massachusetts Institute of Technology, were hired as programmers by a small computer company named Tenet. Woz went back to his old pastimes of attending science fairs and diving into the latest books and magazines on computers. When the summer ended, Alan returned to Massachusetts, but Woz stayed with Tenet and enrolled at the local DeAnza Community College.

Alan often sent him books and pamphlets from MIT, and Woz continued to learn more about computer design. At this time, a computer made by Data General Corporation, called the Nova minicomputer, was gaining attention. Woz fell in love with it. This was the first computer he had seen that looked small enough to sit on a desk. He was very impressed with the fact that more than 100 silicon chips were mounted on a single circuit board. Stephen's father could see how excited his son was and arranged for him to meet the designer of the latest computer chip, built by a company called Fairchild Semiconductors. The engineer explained to Woz that the number of chips used in a design was certainly important, but the space occupied by the chips on a circuit board mattered just as much. Woz decided that the next computer he designed would not only have as few chips as possible, but the chips themselves would occupy as little space as possible on the board.

Woz got back in touch with his neighborhood friend, Bill Fernendez, and the two resumed their scavenger hunts for electronic components. Although Bill was a few years younger than Woz and still in high school, he was more than happy to help with this new computer project. The first thing Woz did was to call several companies in the valley, *begging* for spare parts. He told each company that he was a penniless student interested in electronics. Several companies cooperated and sent surplus or rejected parts of all shapes and sizes. Woz brought them to Fernendez's house and dumped them on the living room floor. The two boys matched the components with the pictures from each company's catalog.

Bill talked his parents into cleaning out part of their garage so that he and his friend would have a place to work. The two boys spent nearly all summer working nights and weekends in the Fernendez garage, building the computer Woz designed. They drank quarts of cream soda and listened to rock and roll. Because they drank so much cream soda, they decided to call their computer the "Cream Soda Computer." The computer didn't do much more than simple arithmetic, but to Woz it was the first step to his dream come true.

When the boys finished building the computer, Woz's mother was so excited and proud that she called the *San Jose Mercury* newspaper and told reporters about the new computer her 19-year-old son had built. A reporter and photographer came down to look at the machine. Unfortunately, when Woz turned on the computer, a shower of sparks appeared and smoke poured from the machine! Woz just laughed. He knew right away the accident was due to a faulty chip, not his design.

The reporter and photographer left without a story or a picture. But Woz didn't mind. He wasn't after fame or fortune. He just wanted to get his computer to work, so back to work he went.

One day Fernendez ran into a friend from high school, Steven Jobs. He brought Jobs to the garage to introduce him to Woz and the Cream Soda Computer. Jobs was 15 years old, 5 years younger than Woz. He had long, scraggly hair and went barefoot most of the time. Jobs was outgoing and quite eccentric, while Woz was quiet and more of a loner. The two seemed as different as night and day. Yet they found they had a lot in common.

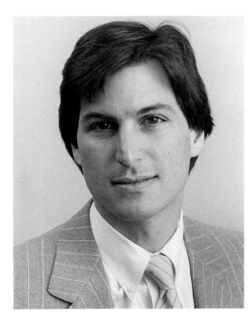

Steve Jobs

Jobs was also interested in electronics, although not to the extent that Woz was, and they both shared a love for practical jokes. Despite differences in character, Woz and Jobs became good friends. They didn't know at that time that their friendship would bring them millions and revolutionize the world of computers.

The two Steves at work on their first business venture—the
blue box.

The Two Steves

After just one year at DeAnza Community College, Woz decided to transfer to the University of California at Berkeley to study engineering. Woz had little time or interest in the protests against the Vietnam War occurring on campus nearly every day. He was far more interested in the "electronics revolution" around him.

One day in October 1971, Woz's mother saw an article in *Esquire* magazine called "Secrets of the Little Blue Box." She thought the story would interest her son. It told of an "outlaw gang" of electronics wizards who figured out how to access the telephone company's computer and make free phone calls with the aid of an electronic box they built and painted blue. A member of the telephone gang, known as "Captain Crunch," had discovered that a prize whistle found in a Cap'n Crunch cereal box tooted the exact tone of the phone company's computer. When the whistle was blown into a telephone receiver, the computer released a long distance line.

Woz read the article and decided he wanted to build a blue box himself. He went to the library, studied phone company manuals, and went to work. He called his friend Steve Jobs and told him about the blue box prank. Jobs loved the idea. The two Steves decided to start their first business venture—building and selling blue boxes. They sold the boxes by word of mouth or door-to-door at Berkeley dormitories for about $100 each. Although it was illegal to use the blue box, Woz and Jobs had fun pulling pranks with it. They eventually sold about 200 boxes before they decided to quit almost two years later.

Woz really wanted to work for Hewlett-Packard, an electronics company in the valley. Hewlett-Packard (HP) had a laid-back atmosphere and a casual dress code. All the employees—and the owners of the company—were addressed by their first names. At the time, HP was exploring new ways to make electronic components as small as possible for use in the handheld calculators they manufactured. By now, Woz's friend Alan Baum worked at HP, and he helped Woz get a job in the Advanced Products Division. Woz dropped out of Berkeley and started designing calculator chips for the company.

Woz moved into his own apartment in Cupertino and was quite happy in the working world, although he never lost his sense of humor. He started a Dial-a-Joke service. He made recordings of several jokes. When a caller dialed the number, Woz's recorded voice would tell a 15-second joke, or he would answer the phone and read a joke from a book. One day a young woman named Alice Robertson called. Woz liked the sound of her voice, so he decided to tease her a little. He said, "I bet I can hang up the phone faster than you can," and quickly hung up. A few minutes later, the woman called back and the two had a conversation, which eventually led to a date. A year later, Woz and Alice married.

At his first full-time job, Woz designed calculator chips for Hewlett-Packard.

Pong

Woz continued his work at Hewlett-Packard during the day and pursued his own projects at night. He designed and built a TV typewriter (a video display with a keyboard) and a modem—an electronic device that allows a computer to communicate with another computer through a telephone line. Woz was able to access a local company's large computer from home and play computer games on it. Nearly every night after work, Woz would spend hours hooked in to computers all over the country. He learned more and more about programming software.

Meanwhile, Steve Jobs had found a job at a video game company called Atari. Home video games were becoming very popular. Atari's success came with an electronic Ping-Pong game called Pong. Woz saw Pong in a bowling alley and instantly became hooked on the game. He thought to himself, "I can program that," and went home to make his own version of Pong. He showed it to Nolan Bushnell, Jobs's boss at Atari. Bushnell was very impressed by the small number of chips Woz used (about 30, compared to Atari's 150). A few weeks later, Bushnell showed Jobs his idea for a new game called Breakout. He offered to pay Jobs and Woz $700 if they could design and program the game for Atari using less than 50 chips. Since Jobs was getting ready for a trip to Oregon, he talked Woz into designing and writing the program in just four days. Woz gladly did so (using 44 chips). They turned the game over to Atari and split the $700. This experience proved once again that the two Steves could work well together and succeed.

Woz and Jobs hold up the board for the Apple I, the computer
that changed the industry forever.

The Homebrew Computer Club

In January 1975, the cover of *Popular Electronics* magazine displayed the headline "World's First Minicomputer Kit..." and showed a picture of a small black box with several switches and lights on its front. The box bore the name "Altair 8800." A small company in Albuquerque, New Mexico, called MITS sold the kit to make the Altair computer for only $399.

When the article came out, the company immediately got orders for hundreds of kits to be shipped by mail. People with less patience drove to New Mexico and camped out in the MITS parking lot, waiting for their kits to be packaged and ready.

Building the Altair computer from a kit wasn't easy, though. First, all of the components had to be sorted and all the computer chips had to be tested (often, many were found to be unusable).

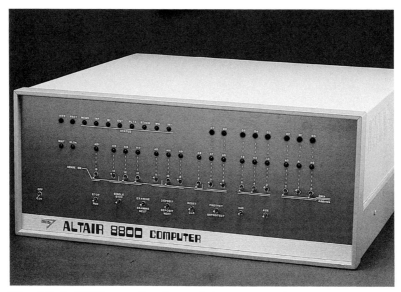

The Altair 8800 was the first minicomputer that could be built from a kit.

Finally, all the pieces had to be soldered (joined with molten metal) onto a circuit board (or a couple of boards) with the aid of only a few pages of instructions. There was no keyboard, no video display, or any way of programming the computer other than flicking the switches on the front panel on and off. For the Altair to be useful, it needed to be attached to a TV screen or video display, a keyboard, extra memory chips, and instruction programs. Adding all of those devices to the $399 kit brought the price of an Altair computer closer to $3,000.

The attraction of the Altair computer, however, was the new kind of computer chip it used—a *microprocessor*. The microprocessor used in the Altair computer, called the 8080 chip, was quite different from the chips used in minicomputers. Minicomputers used several dozen chips, each designed to perform a single task, soldered together on one or more circuit boards. A microprocessor chip, or "microchip," could perform *several* functions on its own, *without* having to be soldered to additional chips or additional boards. This new technology was gaining a lot of attention. Soon electronics companies began manufacturing different models of microchips.

Woz didn't see the ad for the Altair 8800 in *Popular Electronics* until several months after it came out. But he did find a group of people who shared his dream.

His friend Alan Baum had seen a notice posted on a tree at Stanford University. The notice read:

AMATEUR COMPUTER USERS GROUP. HOME-BREW COMPUTER CLUB...you name it. Are you building your own computer? Terminal? TV typewriter? ... If so, you might like to come to a gathering of people with like-minded interests. Exchange information, swap ideas, help work on a project, whatever....

Alan knew immediately that this club would be perfect for his friend Stephen Wozniak. But he also knew that because Woz could be shy, he might not be willing to attend a meeting with a room full of strangers. So Alan told Woz the meeting was for people who designed TV terminals, and since Woz had designed one, he should go to the club to see what was new.

Thirty-two people showed up for the meeting, including Woz and Baum. Some of the people knew each other, but all 32 attendees had at least one thing in common: the desire to build and own a computer of their very own. Six of the 32 had built their own computer system of some sort, while several others awaited their Altair kits. One person brought in his Altair, which he proudly showed off in front of the room.

At first, Woz felt out of place. He hadn't even heard of the Altair computer kit. But he began to feel at home when several people talked about the computers they "home-brewed" on their own, similar to the Cream Soda Computer Woz had built a few years earlier. Woz knew then he wasn't alone in his quest anymore. The biweekly Homebrew Computer Club meetings became one of the highlights of Woz's life.

Woz brought home the microprocessor data sheet that someone had passed out to the club members. He spent all night studying it. He quickly realized that the only difference between this new kind of computer built around a microchip and the minicomputers he had known so well since high school was their size. All he had to do was think smaller, and he could easily design, build, and program a computer around this new microprocessor technology.

Woz told his friend Steve Jobs about the club and he too started attending the meetings. Woz sat in the back of the room, too shy to ever raise his hand, and just listened to all of the computer news and gossip around him. But he still had a major problem—money. He couldn't afford to buy an Altair computer kit. Even the chips themselves, although they were becoming cheaper, were still too costly for Woz to buy at nearly $200 apiece.

Around this time, Woz attended the Wescom computer show in San Francisco. A company called MOS Technology was selling old models of their new microchip, the 6502, for only $20. Thrilled at the price, Woz immediately bought a handful. He decided then that the 6502 chip would be the heart of his own computer. Before designing the computer, however, Woz wrote the programming language he wanted his computer to run. The most popular programming language at the time was BASIC. But he wanted a BASIC that offered more than the one that was available, so he sat down and wrote his own. He called it the WOZ INTEGER BASIC. When Woz's friends at the club heard that Woz wrote a language for a computer that didn't exist yet, they were more than impressed.

Once the BASIC was written, the only thing left for Woz to do was design and build the computer for it to run on. That was the easy part, Woz felt, since he had already designed several computers in the past and had even built one. Within a few weeks, his computer was complete. He soldered one of his small TV terminals right onto the board. The board also contained "interfaces," or hookups, to connect it to a keyboard, a power supply, and a video display. Once everything was hooked up, he could sit down and program his computer to do something interesting, like play a game! Woz wasn't thinking of a computer to sell, but one to have fun with.

Woz brought his computer board to Homebrew and passed out copies of his design so that others could copy it. Some of the people at Homebrew were impressed, some offered suggestions for improvements, but nearly everyone questioned his decision to build his computer around a chip different than the one used by the very popular Altair computer. By now most of the Homebrew members were writing programs or designing new boards to connect with the Altair. Why use a 6502 chip instead of the 8080, the group wanted to know. It was a matter of price, Woz replied, nothing more.

But there was another substantial difference. Woz's computer had the same capabilities of an Altair with several additional boards connected to it. Woz's computer was built using only one board. The board was about the size of a piece of paper, with about 30 to 40 chips neatly arranged on it.

The two Steves built the Apple I in Jobs's garage.

Steve Jobs immediately saw the potential for something big. He noticed that some people at the club were interested in Woz's machine. He and Woz even went to some members' homes to help them build a Woz machine of their own. Jobs had the idea of selling a computer board based on Woz's design. "Let's start a company," Jobs said.

Woz had never dreamed of selling his invention. He simply designed and built it for fun, and to impress his friends at the club. But Jobs kept pushing. There were now 500 people in the club. If he and Woz could make the board for $25 and sell it for $40 to just 50 people, they could get their money back and even make a few dollars. Woz seemed doubtful at first, but he finally agreed that as long as he wouldn't have to quit his job at HP, he'd work after hours with Jobs and start a company. Jobs suggested they name the computer "Apple," remembering his past summer days working on an apple orchard in Oregon. "It'll be fun, just like the old blue box days!" he said. "For once in our lives we'll have a real company!" Woz was 25 years old. Jobs was 20.

Since Woz was a loyal HP employee, he thought he should first check with the company to see if they wanted to sell the Apple computer. He brought the Apple to his supervisors at HP. They thought it was a fine machine, but that it just didn't fit in with the company's product line. They simply weren't interested in what they felt was just a "hobby market." Woz got a legal release from HP to build and sell the machine on his own time.

Woz and Jobs sold their most valuable possessions in order to start their venture. Woz sold his HP calculator and Jobs sold his Volkswagen van, which gave them a total of about $1,300. Jobs talked his parents into giving them working space in their garage, and just like that, Apple Computer Company was born.

Apple Computer Company's first logo

Woz proudly displays the Apple I board.

48

Apple Computer Company

No one, least of all the two Steves, could have guessed what the future would hold for Apple Computer Company. Stephen Wozniak wanted to build a computer an engineer would love to own. Steven Jobs had the vision and drive to sell that computer to everyone in the world. On April Fools' Day of 1976, the two Steves signed an agreement about their newly formed company. Woz would be in charge of designing and creating the machine and Jobs would be in charge of selling it.

At a Homebrew meeting in July 1976, Woz and Jobs formally demonstrated the Apple computer to the whole group. Woz answered questions from members and listened to their suggestions about features to add. If someone had an idea he liked, he would add the feature to his computer and bring it to the next meeting to show off again.

But Jobs wasn't going to stop at just that. He had another idea brewing in the back of his mind. He noticed that a man by the name of Paul Terrell was attending the club meetings. Terrell owned a retail computer store called The Byte Shop. He had just started selling Altair computer kits in his shop. During one Homebrew meeting, Jobs gave Terrell a private demonstration of the Apple computer. Jobs asked him if he would like to sell the Apple computer board at his store. Terrell said he might be interested and told Jobs to keep in touch.

The very next day, Jobs went down to The Byte Shop and talked to Terrell again. Terrell was impressed with Jobs's perseverance. He told Jobs he would order up to 100 computers, but only if they were fully assembled and tested, not just the plug-in boards. Terrell also told Jobs that the computers must be delivered within 30 days. Terrell said he would pay between $400 and $500 apiece for the computers. Jobs tried to conceal screams of excitement and immediately called Woz at HP to tell him the good news. Woz couldn't believe it when Jobs told him about the $50,000 order. He would later say it was the most exhilarating day in the history of Apple Computer Company. "Nothing was ever so great and so unexpected," he said.

Jobs thought they should build 200 computer boards, sell half to The Byte Shop, and reserve 100 to sell on their own to club members or by advertising in electronics magazines. He decided the retail price of the computer should be $666.66.

An early poster
for the Apple II

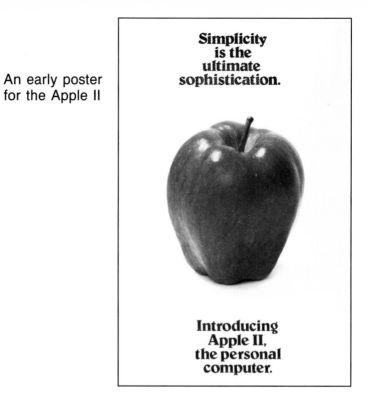

There was one thing, however, that the two hadn't prepared for: the cost of building 100 fully assembled machines. They needed money to buy the parts to fill the order! Neither Jobs nor Woz had the money or even knew where to start to look for it.

Jobs began by going to banks and asking for loans. All the banks he went to flatly refused what they thought were two crazy kids with a far-out idea. Next he tried to find electronics companies in the valley willing to sell parts on credit. He finally found a company in Palo Alto willing to sell Apple the needed parts, with payment due in 30 days. So with parts in hand, the two Steves set out to assemble 100 Apple computers. Twenty-nine days after the order from Paul Terrell, Jobs and Woz delivered the computers to The Byte Shop.

Woz continued to go to Homebrew meetings, attempting to impress fellow members with his computer's latest features. One of the first things he did was add a color video display, which gave the computer a very different and impressive look. Woz also added a casette-tape interface to the machine. Now the user could load the BASIC programming language automatically from a tape, rather than having to type it all in by hand. He also found ways to make the machine run much faster with about half the number of microchips. He called this new, improved computer the Apple II.

Woz added these features so that he could play Breakout, the game he had previously designed for Atari, on his own computer. Woz later said that it was the most satisfying day of his life when he went to Homebrew and demonstrated Breakout on his computer. A couple of Woz's friends from the club, Randy Wigginton and Chris Espinosa, demonstrated some other games they had written in BASIC for Woz's Apple computer.

Meanwhile, Jobs kept looking for more money for the new company. Through several connections, Jobs met businessman Mike Markkula. Markkula had a few meetings with the two Steves. He gave them advice on how to organize Apple and eventually wrote a business plan for the company. After seeing the computer in action, Markkula decided to invest his own money to get the company going. He agreed that home computers might really turn into something big. There was one catch. Markkula would only agree to the venture if Woz quit his job at HP and gave Apple 100 percent of his attention.

Woz wasn't easily convinced. He liked his job at HP. He liked the steady paychecks. He was afraid that designing computers full-time might not be as fun as it was in Jobs's garage or at Homebrew. Mostly, he didn't want the responsibility of running a company. His wife, Alice, wasn't so keen on the idea, either. Their marriage had already begun to suffer from the amount of time Woz spent working on computers. Alice was afraid that if Woz devoted all of his time and priorities to Apple, they would have even less time together. Woz told Jobs and Markkula that his answer was no. But they didn't accept his answer and spent hours and hours talking to Woz. They promised that he wouldn't have to run the company. Finally, Woz agreed to quit his job at HP and make Apple Computer his number-one priority.

The first official employee of Apple Computer was Bill Fernendez, Woz's friend who had introduced the two Steves to each other. Jobs also hired Randy Wigginton and Chris Espinosa to write more software for the Apple. Markkula hired a man named Mike Scott to be Apple's first president, responsible for running day-to-day operations.

By January 1977, Apple Computer had established its first office on Stevens Creek Boulevard, a few miles from Homestead High School in Cupertino. Desks and work benches were brought in from Jobs's garage. The first few days, Woz, Jobs, Fernendez, Wigginton, and Espinosa sat in different parts of the office, playing a game with the telephones. Each tried to buzz someone else's phone first. None of them realized how soon the phones would be ringing off the hook with people anxious to buy Apple computers.

The initial task for the new company was to prepare for the first West Coast Computer Faire coming in April. The two Steves wanted to officially introduce the Apple II to the world. The crew worked day and night, soldering, designing, and programming.

Woz seemed to be working 24 hours a day to finish all of his enhancements to the Apple II. His home life began to suffer even more. Before long, his marriage with Alice ended in divorce.

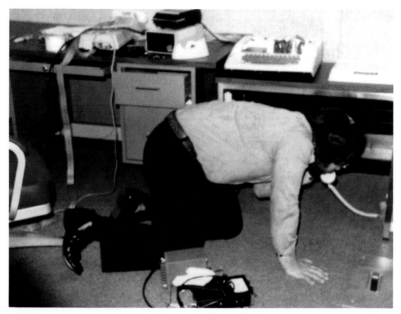

Phones at the Apple offices rang off the hook with people wanting to buy their own Apple II computers.

Jobs had ideas of his own for improving the machine. He thought that instead of the typical dark metal boxes that housed most early computers, the Apple II computer should look completely different—*friendly.* He covered the computer with a lightweight, beige plastic case that brought the keyboard and computer together in a sleek design. Not one screw or bolt was visible. The machine looked like some kind of typewriter from the future. Woz wanted the computer to work perfectly, but he could have cared less about what it looked like. For Jobs, on the other hand, size and the simplicity of the machine's appearance mattered just as much as its function. Two of his favorite mottoes were "Don't trust a computer you can't lift," and "A computer that is easy to use will be used more often." Both could be said about the new Apple II.

The West Coast Computer Faire was a huge success for Apple. Jobs arranged to have the biggest and most elegant booth at the Faire. He pasted the company's new logo—a multicolored, striped apple with a bite taken out of it—on the booth.

The Apple II was introduced to the world at the West Coast Computer Faire.

He brought in a large projection screen to demonstrate programs and placed the company's only four Apple II computers on either side of the booth. Jobs, Mike Scott, Chris Espinosa, and Randy Wigginton worked at the booth while Mike Markkula walked around the exhibition hall signing up dealers for the company.

By the end of 1977, Apple Computer had earned $2 million in sales of Apple II computers. Business was booming. One day during a meeting in December 1977, Mike Markkula complained that his favorite program for balancing his checkbook took a long time to read into the computer from the cassette tape. That was all it took to send Woz off in a new direction. The following week Woz and Randy Wigginton spent the entire week, including the holidays, working on something they called a flexible disk drive. The drive would read programs from a floppy diskette, instead of the clumsy cassette tape. Not only would it increase speed, but the disk drive would also add a feature to the Apple II that no other computer had! Woz said later that designing the disk drive for the Apple was his most incredible experience at Apple and the finest job he ever did. The chip that controlled the disk drive is still used in the Apple's line of Macintosh computers. It is called the IWM chip, which stands for Incredible Woz Machine.

When Apple began shipping the disk drive to stores in June 1978, the company took off like a rocket. People were thrilled by the new floppy disk drive. Now more complex programs could be stored on floppy disks. "Serious" software such as word processors and business programs appeared in computer stores. People weren't just buying computers to play games or write programs. An entire new set of customers, mostly businesspeople, began buying Apple computers. They didn't have to know how to write their own programs. More and more companies got into the business of programming and selling software for the Apple II computer. The "software industry" had arrived.

During Apple's third year, the company sold 100,000 Apple II computers. By 1980 sales were up to $139 million, and by 1981, $583 million. Apple Computer ended the 1980s as the largest supplier of personal computers in the United States. By December 1980, more than 40 Apple employees and investors were millionaires. Never before had one company made so many people so rich so quickly. Stephen Wozniak, at the age of 30, was suddenly worth $88 million. He gave a lot of money to his parents and siblings, and also to Alice, his ex-wife. Woz set up the "Woz Plan," so that employees could buy Apple stock at a reduced price from Woz himself.

Woz was a millionaire many times over by the time he celebrated his 30th birthday.

Woz discovered he was wealthy beyond his dreams. He bought a "cute little tiny copper Porsche" and a beautiful house on 26 acres of land in the hills of Los Gatos, overlooking the Silicon Valley. Parts of the house were built to look like an authentic limestone cave, with fake dinosaur footprints, fossils, and prehistoric rock carvings. Woz set up one room entirely for video games, computers, and wall-to-wall television screens. He also bought himself a single-engine four-seater airplane, called a Beachcraft Bonanza, and he earned his pilot's license.

Woz has loved airplanes since he was a kid. Here he gets a ride in an air force jet.

He began dating Candi Clark, an ex-Olympic kayak racer who worked as a financial analyst at Apple. One day in February 1981, Woz and Candi were about to fly to San Diego in Woz's Bonanza when the plane crashed on takeoff. Candi suffered numerous broken bones in her face and a shattered finger. Woz suffered a head injury that affected his short-term memory. He remembered things from the long-ago past, but nothing from his recent past. Five weeks later, Woz recovered completely, but he never got those lost memories back.

Four months after the crash, in June of 1981, Woz and Candi were married in Candi's home. One of their favorite singers, Emmy Lou Harris, sang at the reception. They lived in the 26-acre Santa Cruz mountain home with pets that included Siberian huskies, donkeys, a red-tailed hawk, and more than 60 llamas.

By this time, Apple had more than 100 engineers and was running well on its own. Apple introduced the Macintosh computer, which would later replace the Apple II line, becoming the mainstay of Apple Computer Company.

Woz thought it might be a good time to take some time off from Apple. He wanted to go back to college. He reenrolled at Berkeley, continuing his studies in computer science and engineering. He also took a lot of classes in psychology and memory, to try and understand what happened to him during the five weeks he suffered from amnesia.

Woz makes a friend during a vacation in Australia.

Life after Apple

One day in 1982, Woz was driving along the highway listening to his car radio, and he heard a string of songs by a bunch of his favorite musical groups. He wondered why popular musical groups never play on stage one after another, just like on the radio. He decided to put on a great outdoor rock festival. As usual, all of his effort and energy went into creating the best rock festival possible.

The first thing he did was form a company called Unuson (which stands for Unite Us in Song), dedicated to promoting rock concerts and "a new kind of unity." Woz wanted to unite the world of technology with the world of rock and roll. He wanted to introduce young America to technology. Woz flew his plane all around southern California to find the perfect spot for this outdoor event. He decided on a place in Devore, California, near the San Bernardino Mountains. He spent weeks talking with rock musicians and booking groups for the three-day show, planned for the 1982 Labor Day weekend. Music groups and singers including

Fleetwood Mac, the Police, the Grateful Dead, Tom Petty, Jackson Browne, Chick Corea, and Herbie Hancock all agreed to perform. Woz called the three-day rock concert—with a computer fair as a sideshow—the "US Festival." He said, "Maybe we can realize that one of the ways to take care of ourselves is to think of all of us as a whole." Unuson made a film of the festival's theme to distribute free to more than 4,000 schools around the world, along with a curriculum to help teachers discuss it with students.

The first US Festival

During the festival, Woz walked through the huge crowds of nearly 400,000 people and talked to as many as he could. "Are you having a good time?" he asked. "Any problems?" Nearly all of the people told Woz they were having a great time, thanking him endlessly for the event. The musicians played one after another on a huge stage. Off to the side of the stage was a tented area filled with computers and video games. People could explore what was new in the world of computing, or just hang out in the air-conditioned rooms and play computer games. The latest Apple II computers were the stars, of course. In one tent, selected speakers talked to as many as 500 people. Herbie Hancock, a popular jazz keyboardist, told a full tent how he used the Apple computer to store music and how he wrote programs to help keep his accounts straight when he was on the road. He also talked about different kinds of music-notation software.

As a treat to all the fans, on September 3, Woz brought out on stage his first son, Jesse John Clark, born that day. Woz said that he and Candi decided to give their son Candi's last name, since it was easier to spell than Wozniak.

Woz had such a great time at the festival that he decided to put on another US Festival the following year, once again on Labor Day weekend.

Woz met many of his favorite musicians, such as Emmy Lou Harris, at the US Festivals.

Again, the festival was a success in terms of the music, the organized crowd, and, as Woz said, the "great time had by all!" Woz was a little surprised and discouraged, however, at how little some of the performers cared about the theme of cooperation and sharing. Very few seemed to share in the "US philosophy." He decided he would not put on another US Festival in the near future.

In the spring of 1983, Woz went to an Apple Computer Company picnic. He talked with Apple's president, John Scully. Scully told Woz that the company missed him terribly and asked him to come back for a time. Woz agreed, but only if he could remain an engineer and not have to get involved in management. He showed up the following day to a standing ovation from everyone in the company.

In 1985 Woz decided to go on to something new. He was having a problem at home, a problem that he called "laptop clutter." So Woz left Apple and formed a company called "Cloud 9" to solve his "laptop clutter" problem. Woz explained, "I wanted a computer, so I designed the Apple. I live in a house with lots of televisions and VCRs, and I wanted a single unit to control them all, so I formed Cloud 9."

Woz designed a universal remote-control device to replace all the individual remote-control units. The device also included a clock and a timer for recording TV programs. Woz stayed busy with this for a while, and then in 1986 he joined Cloud 9 with Nolan Bushnell's latest company. Bushnell's company manufactured talking stuffed bears and other high-technology toys. Woz had always been fascinated with toys and children. By now he and Candi had another child, Sarah Nadine, born in 1984. Woz and Bushnell started a company called Tech Force, which manufactured toy robots run by remote-control devices. They said their company was "dedicated to teaching children of all ages to live with and love technology."

A few years later, Woz and Candi divorced. Woz took some time out from the working world and pursued hobbies such as learning to play the piano. He also spent some time in Mexico learning the Spanish language and about the culture. Then he moved to Los Gatos, California, and began volunteering in a kindergarten classroom.

Woz now lives with his third wife, Suzanne, who is an attorney, and their joined family of six children: Adam, Daniel, Marcy, Jesse, Sarah, and Gary. Woz says, "The joy I get playing with my kids is equal to the joy I got designing computers." He teaches computers in a small elementary school in the Santa Cruz mountains, where three of his children (Jesse, Sarah, and Gary) have attended. He says of his teaching, "I'm trying to give kids an advantage with computer instruction."

Woz has a friendly relationship with Apple. He lets the company know excitedly about what he is doing in his own teaching. He and his son Jesse posed for an advertisement for the newest line of computers, Macintosh Powerbook.

Woz also does a lot of public speaking these days and enjoys it very much—quite a change from the person who was too shy to raise his hand in the Homebrew Computer Club meetings! He feels fortunate that he learned about public speaking from the ground up, first speaking to amateur engineers in the Homebrew Computer Club, then later to professional computer clubs and his company, and then to larger gatherings of people.

Woz still feels that humor is very important in life. "Playing jokes, making jokes, and telling a joke is my idea of the greatest type of creativity." And creativity is the essence of everything Stephen Wozniak has done and will venture to do in the years ahead. That's the Woz, a true pie-in-ear!

GLOSSARY

BASIC: **B**eginner's **A**ll-purpose **S**ymbolic Instruction Code—a language for giving a computer instructions. Some other computer languages are COBOL (**CO**mmon **B**usiness **O**riented **L**anguage), FORTRAN (**FOR**mula **TRAN**slation), and Pascal.

board: Boards are the "guts" of a computer. Circuits are etched and printed on boards, and a computer's chips, transistors, and other electrical components are also wired onto boards.

disk drive: a device that holds the floppy disks that a computer reads for information and instructions.

mainframe: a computer that is large in both size and memory. The first computers were mainframes.

microprocessor: an electronic device consisting of thousands of transistors on a tiny silicon chip. Microprocessors—or microchips—also contain some of a computer's memory.

software: programs used by computers to perform specific desired tasks, such as balancing a checkbook or writing a letter.

ACKNOWLEDGMENTS

Photographs used with the permission of Margret Wozniak, courtesy of Unuson except pp. 8, 30, 38, 45, 47, 56, Apple Computer, Inc.; p. 12, IBM; p. 27, University of Colorado Public Relations Office; p. 35, Hewlett-Packard; p. 36, Atari Games Corporation; p. 40, The Smithsonian Institution; pp. 60, 64, 66, Dan Sokol, courtesy of Unuson; pp. 71, 72, Ed Kashi.